Page Turners

Come Home

Sue Leather & Julian Thomlinson

Series Editor: Rob Waring
Story Editor: Julian Thomlinson
Series Development Editor: Sue Leather

Australia • Brazil • Japan • Korea • Mexico • Singapore • Spain • United Kingdom • United States

Page Turners Reading Library

Come Home

Sue Leather & Julian Thomlinson

Publisher: Andrew Robinson

Executive Editor: Sean Bermingham

Senior Development Editor: Derek Mackrell

Assistant Editor: Sarah Tan

Director of Global Marketing: Ian Martin

Content Project Manager: Tan Jin Hock

Print Buyer: Susan Spencer

Layout Design and Illustrations: Redbean Design Pte Ltd

Cover Illustration: Eric Foenander

Photo Credits:
34 DrRave/iStockphoto,
35 JoyBrown/Shutterstock,
36 cartoons/Shutterstock

ISBN-13: 978-1-4240-4662-1

ISBN-10: 1-4240-4662-9

Heinle
20 Channel Center Street
Boston, Massachusetts 02210
USA

Cengage Learning is a leading provider of customized learning solutions with office locations around the globe, including Singapore, the United Kingdom, Australia, Mexico, Brazil, and Japan. Locate your local office at:
international.cengage.com/region

Cengage Learning products are represented in Canada by Nelson Education, Ltd.

Visit Heinle online at **elt.heinle.com**

Visit our corporate website at **www.cengage.com**

Printed in the United States of America
2 3 4 5 6 7 – 14 13 12 11

Contents

People in the story		3
Chapter 1	Come home!	4
Chapter 2	Professor Saunders	9
Chapter 3	A good time	15
Chapter 4	A surprise	21
Chapter 5	Good-byes	27
Review		32
Answer Key		33

Background Reading

Spotlight on... Studying Abroad	34
Spotlight on... Homesickness	36
Glossary	37

BRENTON COLLEGE

People in the story

Samorn Sutapa
Samorn is a student at Brenton College. She comes from Thailand and doesn't like the cold weather.

Lek Metanee
Lek is Samorn's boyfriend. He lives in Thailand.

Ying-Chu Zhang
Ying-Chu is a student at Brenton College. She is in the same dorm as Samorn.

Harrison Morgan
Harrison is a student at Brenton College. He's studying law.

Professor Melanie Saunders
Professor Saunders is coach of the taekwondo team at Brenton College. She helps students with their problems.

Mr. Babic
Mr. Babic is the economics teacher at Brenton College.

This story is set in Brenton, a college town in the northwestern United States.

Chapter 1

Come home!

"OK, that's it for today," says Mr. Babic. "Read some more of your book for the next class."

The students put their books in their bags and start to go out of the classroom. Samorn doesn't get up. She puts her head on the table. *This is very difficult,* she thinks. She loves economics, but here in the USA she has to study it in English. She isn't studying in Thai, her language. It's difficult to understand everything. She looks at the other students in the class. They look happy. *They're happy because they understand,* she thinks.

Samorn closes her eyes and starts to think about home. She thinks about Thailand where she lives. She thinks about the hot weather, about the nice food, and about her friends. She remembers her mother and father, her sisters and brothers. She thinks about her boyfriend Lek and she wants to cry. *Why am I here?* she thinks. This is only her first week at Brenton College, but she wants to go home.

Samorn looks at her watch. It's just after eleven o'clock. In Thailand it's one o'clock in the morning.

She goes out of the classroom and she walks to her room in the dorm. It's nice, but cold. It's September and the trees are orange and brown. She sees students everywhere, in twos and threes. They're laughing and talking as they walk to and from their classes. They all look . . . happy.

"Hi!" Samorn hears someone speaking and she looks. She sees a student from her class. *Harrison, his name is,* she thinks.

"Hello," Samorn replies. She smiles a little, but she doesn't look into Harrison's eyes.

Harrison is with some friends. They're all laughing at Harrison. Harrison is funny and he says funny things. She sees that in class. He's good-looking, too, and he looks rich. He wears good clothes. He comes from a very rich family, she knows. Samorn's family has money too—her mother and father are lawyers in Bangkok—but it's not the same. She's different from him, from all of them. She walks to her dorm room at Evelyn Royce House. She looks at her room and thinks, *Is this really my home for the next four years?*

That evening, Samorn gets a phone call from Lek, her boyfriend back in Bangkok. *I don't want to speak to him now,* she thinks. *I don't want him to know I'm not happy here.* But she talks to him anyway.

"Samorn! How's everything?" he asks her.

"Oh, everything's good. Really good," she tells him.

"Really? Isn't it cold?" he asks her.

"It's cold, yes."

"It's beautiful here today. How about the classes? Can you understand everything?" he asks.

"The classes. Well, they're . . . They're OK," she says. She tries to make her voice happy.

Lek's eating something.

"Are you eating?" she asks him.

"Samorn, it's Friday. I'm having dinner at Lemon Grass. We always come here on Fridays, remember? I'm here, thinking of you," Lek says. Samorn really likes the Lemon Grass restaurant. They make really good food. She meets Lek there for dinner every Friday. She remembers and she starts to cry. She puts the phone away from her face.

"Samorn, are you there? Samorn!"

"I'm here."

"Samorn, you're crying."

"Lek, it's difficult here," she says. "I'm different from the other students! And it's very cold."

"Oh, Samorn," says Lek. "Are you sure you want to be there? You know, you can always come home . . ."

"Please, Lek. I don't want to talk about this again. Not now."

"Everybody here understands . . . ," he goes on.

Samorn knows Lek doesn't want her to stay in America. She knows he wants her to come home.

But what do I want? she thinks.

Chapter 2

Professor Saunders

That night Samorn doesn't sleep much. She hears Lek, saying, "You can always come home." Home. It's a good word. She loves Lek, and she's really unhappy here. *Why not go home?* she thinks. But then she remembers that she's here in the USA because it's a good place to study. She wants to be a lawyer. She wants to study economics and then law. It's good for her future. *But it's really difficult,* she thinks.

The next Monday, Samorn doesn't have any classes, but she gets up early and goes to the college. She goes into the building where the professors have their offices. She walks up to a big door. On the door it says "Professor Melanie Saunders."

Professor Saunders looks after the students and their studies. *I must talk to her about all this,* Samorn thinks. She has to tell the professor that she's unhappy. Samorn puts her hand to the door and knocks on it.

"Come in!" says a big voice.

Samorn opens the door and walks into the professor's room. She sees a big woman in a red tracksuit.

"I run every morning," says the professor. "Before class." She smiles at Samorn.

"Sit down."

Samorn sits down. On the wall, she can see some pictures of Professor Saunders doing taekwondo. The professor is the coach of the college team, too.

"It's Samorn, isn't it? How can I help you?" The professor smiles at Samorn.

She knows my name, thinks Samorn. She starts to talk to the professor. At first, it's slow. Then she talks fast. She talks about her family, then about her studies and coming to the USA. She talks about what she wants to do in the future.

Samorn looks at Professor Saunders. The teacher's listening. Her eyes are big and brown. "I want to study, but I'm unhappy here," Samorn says. "I think I want to go home."

"Mmm," says the professor. She thinks for a minute. Then she takes some papers and starts to read them. After a few minutes she says, "It says here that you are a very good student, Samorn. You have 'A' grades in Thailand."

"Thank you," says Samorn.

"It says that you work a lot," says the professor.

Samorn just looks at Saunders.

"Are you sure about this?" asks Saunders.

"I . . ."

"It's only the first week, Samorn," Saunders goes on. "I know it's not easy for you, but please give it more time."

"I don't know . . . ," says Samorn. Her face looks sad. "It's difficult."

"I understand," says Professor Saunders. "Really, I do. Everything's different here, isn't it?"

"Yes."

"I see a lot of students from Thailand and other countries. . . . The language is difficult . . . You can't eat the food . . . I know."

She really understands, thinks Samorn.

"But this is only the start," says Professor Saunders. "Think about next week, next month, next year . . . You want to be a lawyer and I'm sure you can be a very good lawyer."

"I don't know . . ." says Samorn.

"What do your mother and father think?"

"They are very happy about me being here. They like America very much. But . . ."

"Yes?"

"My boyfriend, Lek."

Samorn remembers the talk with Lek in Bangkok. She remembers his words. "I know you want to study in the USA, Samorn. I understand. But I don't really like it."

"You must think about your future, Samorn. Look, it's October 2nd now. Please try one month, Samorn," says the professor. "Only one more month."

"A month!" says Samorn. Four weeks. "It's too long . . . I can't."

"OK, so please give it one more week, then," says the professor.

Samorn looks at Professor Saunders. The professor is smiling.

"I don't know . . ." Samorn starts.

"Just a week. Come and see me next Monday. Then we can talk."

"My feelings won't change, Professor Saunders."

"OK. Then next week you can go home."

Samorn thinks about it. *Maybe one more week isn't too bad.*

"OK," says Samorn. "A week."

Chapter 3

A good time

Samorn goes out of Professor Saunders' office and out of the building. *A week*, she thinks. *Can I do it?* Then she thinks about going home. About seeing Lek and her family. In only one week! She sends a text message from her phone to Lek. "Coming home next week," it says. Two minutes later the message "Great!" comes back.

One week is not long, Samorn thinks. For the first time that week, Samorn smiles.

"Hey! You look happy today!"

Samorn looks up and sees a Chinese girl in a blue tracksuit. She's running, but stops to speak to Samorn.

"Hi," says Samorn. "You're Ying-Chu, aren't you?"

"That's right," says the girl. "We're in the same class. It's Samorn, isn't it?"

"That's right." *That's two people who know my name*, she thinks.

"What do you think of Mr. Babic?" asks Ying-Chu.

"Oh," smiles Samorn. "He's nice . . ."

"And good-looking too!" Ying-Chu laughs.

Samorn laughs.

"We're in the same dorm too—Evelyn Royce," says Ying-Chu.

"Yes," says Samorn. "That's right."

Ying-Chu looks at her watch. "I must go," she says. "But some of us from the dorm are going out on Wednesday night. Do you want to come?"

"I . . . umm, I don't know," says Samorn.

"Come on," says Ying-Chu. "We're going to a nightclub. It's called The Wheel. It's very good. They have great music for dancing. It's a lot of fun!

Samorn looks at Ying-Chu's smiling face. "OK," she says. *I like dancing,* she thinks. *Why not?*

"Great!" says Ying-Chu. "See you tomorrow. How about 7:30?"

"Great," says Samorn.

"OK. Well, I must finish my run now. See you."

"OK! See you tomorrow," calls Samorn as Ying-Chu runs off.

On Saturday evening, Samorn gets ready to go out with Ying-Chu and the other girls from their dorm. She puts on a beautiful dress and brushes her long black hair. When she's ready, she looks in the mirror. She thinks she looks good.

At 7:30, Ying-Chu comes to Samorn's room.

"Hi, Ying-Chu," says Samorn. "You look different!"

"I'm not in my tracksuit now," says Ying-Chu. She laughs and then says, "You look different, too. You look beautiful, Samorn."

Then Samorn thinks about Lek. "You're beautiful," he always tells her. She smiles when she thinks about that, and about seeing him next week. *Only six days now,* she thinks.

Then some other girls come. "Samorn, this is Fleur, Maria, and Jen." Then she says, "Girls, this is Samorn."

They walk to Brenton and The Wheel nightclub. They talk and laugh as they walk. The girls are nice, thinks Samorn. *But what about the nightclub? Is it different?* This isn't the first time in a nightclub for Samorn, but it's the first time in the USA.

Thirty minutes later they get to the nightclub. They can hear the music before they go in. *I must try to have a good time,* Samorn thinks. *After all, I'm going home next week.*

There are a lot of people at the nightclub—students and people from the city. The music is loud and lots of people are dancing. They all dance on the dance floor. Samorn stays with Ying-Chu.

"Let's dance!" says Ying-Chu and walks to the dance floor. The other girls go with Ying-Chu, but Samorn doesn't go.

"Come on, Samorn!" Ying-Chu runs back and takes Samorn's arm. She pulls her to the dance floor. "It's great!" she says in Samorn's ear. The music is loud and it makes everyone dance. Then, Samorn's dancing, too.

Samorn and the other girls dance. They dance and dance and dance. Samorn looks at her watch. It's eleven o'clock, but she doesn't want to stop. *This is great,* she thinks. *Just like the nightclubs in Bangkok!* Samorn and the girls dance late into the night.

Chapter 4

A surprise

In Thursday's class, Mr. Babic tells the students that they must make a presentation on the American economy.

"Work with a friend," he says. "You have today to read about it and work on the presentation. You give the presentations tomorrow."

Mr. Babic puts the students into twos. Samorn wants to work with Ying-Chu, but Mr. Babic puts her with Harrison.

"OK," says Harrison. "Let's do it." He smiles at her.

He's nice, she thinks. "OK," she says. She takes out the book. "Why don't you start the presentation, and I finish it?"

"OK," says Harrison, smiling.

Samorn starts to read, but the language is a little difficult for her.

"Everything OK?" asks Harrison.

"Umm . . . What does this mean?" she asks.

Harrison tells her. He helps her with her English as they work on their presentation. He works a lot, but he's funny, and he makes Samorn laugh, too. *But what about giving the presentation?* she thinks. *What about her*

English? She wants to be good. After all, one day she wants to be a lawyer, and lawyers need to speak well. She tells Harrison she's worried.

"Don't worry," he tells her. "I can help you."

They work all day and all evening.

The next day, Samorn and Harrison go to class. They are giving their presentation. Harrison starts. He speaks well and Mr. Babic looks happy. Then Samorn speaks. She feels a little worried as she starts to speak to all the class. She doesn't want to speak badly. But after a minute she sees everyone is listening to her. They are smiling at her. Soon she feels good. Her voice is strong now.

"Thank you for listening to our presentation," she finishes.

"Great!" the students say and clap their hands.

"Very good," says Mr. Babic. "Good work, Samorn. Good work, Harrison."

After the class, Harrison speaks to Samorn.

"You're great, Samorn. Listen, anytime you need help with English, just ask. Anytime, just ask."

"That's great. Thanks, Harrison," says Samorn, smiling, but then she thinks, *I'm not here next week.*

Thank You for Listening
Samorn
&
Harrison

That night, in her room, Samorn thinks about her week . . . She thinks about Ying-Chu and about dancing at the nightclub. She likes Ying-Chu and she likes the other girls, too. Then she thinks about her presentation with Harrison. Now she has two friends, she thinks—Ying-Chu and Harrison. They're nice. *Maybe it isn't bad here,* she thinks. *Maybe* . . . She gets up and phones Lek.

"Samorn! We're really happy that you're coming home," says Lek. "Do you have everything ready?"

"Lek . . ."

Lek hears something in her voice. "What is it?" he asks.

"I think I want to try it here for one more month," she says.

"A month?" he asks.

"I need to give it more time. Just to see. It isn't bad here now . . ."

He doesn't say anything for some time. "Is it really just a month, Samorn?"

Now Samorn doesn't speak for a minute.

"I don't know . . . ," says Samorn.

"I really miss you," says Lek. "I miss you very much."

"I miss you, too, Lek. I do. But it's not as difficult . . . ," Samorn says. "This week . . . My studies are going well, and . . ."

"You're not coming back, are you?" he asks.

"I don't know," says Samorn. "I'm sorry."

"I need to think about this, Samorn," says Lek. She can hear he's unhappy. "I must go now."

"Lek, wait," says Samorn.

"I love you," he says, and then he's not there.

The next Monday, Samorn goes to see Professor Saunders and tells her that she wants to be at Brenton College for the month.

"I'm very happy to hear that, Samorn," says the professor.

"Thanks," says Samorn. She's happy, too, but she's thinking about Lek. How is he? How does he feel? She knows he's unhappy. Later she tries to phone Lek again, but she can't get him on the phone. *I hope he's OK*, she thinks.

The next morning, there's someone at Samorn's door. It's only eight o'clock. *Who can it be?* thinks Samorn. She goes to the door and opens it. She sees Lek with his bags.

"Lek!" she says. He puts his arms around her and they kiss.

"It really is cold, isn't it?" he says.

"Lek . . . What . . . What are you doing here?"

Lek puts his hand in his coat, takes out a small box and opens it. In it there's a ring.

"Samorn," says Lek, "Samorn, I want you to marry me."

Chapter 5

Good-byes

Samorn and Lek sit in Samorn's room. They talk for a long time.

"I love you, Samorn," says Lek. "But this is too difficult. It hurts a lot. I know it hurts you, too. Come home with me, back to Bangkok. You can study there and we can marry."

"I love you too, Lek," says Samorn. She looks at her boyfriend. *I love him,* she thinks, *but what about my new life here? What about my studies?*

"Hello!" Samorn hears a girl's voice. Her door opens a little. "It's me—Ying-Chu."

"Come in," says Samorn.

Ying-Chu comes into the room. She's going for her morning run, and she's wearing a tracksuit. When she comes into the room she sees Lek. "Oh," she says. "I can come back later."

"No, it's OK, Ying-Chu," says Samorn. "This is Lek."

"Hi," Ying-Chu smiles at him.

"My boyfriend," says Samorn. "From Thailand."

"Oh . . . I see," says Ying-Chu. Then she says to

Samorn. "It's about tomorrow. We're going to The Wheel again if you want to come. 7:30."

Samorn wants to go to the nightclub. But she looks at Lek and says, "I . . . uh . . . , I don't know . . . I'll talk to you later, OK?"

"OK," says Ying-Chu. "Bye. Bye, Lek." Samorn takes Ying-Chu to the door. "Very good-looking," says Ying-Chu.

Samorn smiles at Ying-Chu and closes the door.

"You're going to nightclubs?" asks Lek.

"No," says Samorn, "Well, yes, but . . ."

"But what? Do you see other men there, Samorn?" he asks.

"It isn't like that!"

"Really? I understand now," says Lek.

"Lek!"

"I'm sorry, Samorn," says Lek. "I'm just tired, and . . . it just hurts, you know?"

"I know," says Samorn. "Why don't you rest a little? We can talk later."

Lek lies down and goes to sleep. Samorn goes out. She wants to think. She walks around the college. She thinks about her new life here. She thinks about her new friends. She thinks about her studies. She thinks about Professor Saunders, and her kind words. *I know I can be a good lawyer if I study here,* she thinks. She walks for a long time. *But I love Lek. Oh, why is it difficult?*

Samorn goes back to her room to see Lek.

"I want to stay," she says.

They talk again. They talk for a long time.

"I understand," says Lek. He's sad, but his voice is strong. "But it can't work."

"We can try, Lek," says Samorn. "We can . . ."

"I love you, Samorn," says Lek. "But I know that if you don't come home, we are finished."

"But why?" says Samorn. "I can come back next year for a week or two—for a vacation."

"It's too long to wait, and it's only two weeks!" says Lek. "Before, in Thailand . . . Well, now I know how it feels, Samorn. I know how much it hurts without you."

"We can try," says Samorn.

"But it's four years, Samorn!" says Lek, "Four years of telephone calls. It can't work like that."

"But . . ."

"I don't want to watch as you go from me little by little . . . ," he says.

"But I'm not!"

"Samorn, you know I'm right," says Lek as he looks into her eyes. "I know you do."

His voice is kind, but he looks very sad.

"No!" says Samorn. She's crying. "You can't do this."

Lek holds Samorn for a long time. She knows he's right. She understands. But it hurts.

Samorn and Lek are at the airport. She's crying. She's trying to be strong, but it's difficult. Very difficult.

"Can we be friends?" she asks him. "Please tell me we can be friends."

He smiles at her sadly.

"Sure, Samorn," he says, and puts his arms around her. He puts his arms around her for a long time. Now Lek is also crying, she sees.

"Lek . . . ," she begins.

"Don't forget me," he says, then kisses her and walks away.

"Oh, Lek," she cries. She can't say anything more. She watches him as he walks to his plane. He doesn't look back again.

Samorn is at the airport for a long time. She goes to the café and watches the planes. She's crying. She sees a big plane. *Is that Lek's plane?* It goes into the blue sky. It's very big. Then it's small. Then it's very small. Then it isn't there.

Samorn looks away. Then she goes out of the café and walks slowly out of the airport. She goes to the train station and she gets on the train back to Brenton College. She sits on the train and looks out at the trees and the sky. She isn't crying now. She's thinking about tomorrow.

Review

A. Match the characters in the story to their descriptions.

1. ____ Lek		**a**. This person invites Samorn dancing.
2. ____ Harrison		**b.** The coach of the Brenton taekwondo team
3. ____ Melanie Saunders		**c.** Samorn's boyfriend
4. ____ Ying-Chu		**d.** The economics teacher
5. ____ Samorn		**e.** This person helps Samorn with her English.
6. ____ Mr. Babic		**f.** This person misses home a lot.

B. Complete the summary using the words in the box.

nightclub	dormitory	marry	lawyer
future	presentation	different	

It is Samorn Sutapa's first week at Brenton College, but she is already thinking of going back to Thailand. She is not happy there because she feels **1.** ________ from everyone else. Her boyfriend Lek wants her to come home, too. But Samorn knows she's in the U.S. to study hard and become a **2.** ________. She talks to Professor Saunders about her problems and what she wants to do in the **3.** ________. The professor tells her to stay in Brenton for just one more week. Samorn feels happier.

Many things happen in one week. She makes friends with Ying-Chu who lives in the same **4.** ________. She also goes dancing at a **5.** ________ with her new friends. In class, Samorn does very well in her **6.** ________ with Harrison. She decides to stay for one more month. But Lek is not happy and he surprises Samorn by visiting her. He asks her to **7.** ________ him, but Samorn says no. In the end, she decides to stay in the U.S. and they break up.

C. Choose the best answer for each question.

1. Why does Samorn want to go home?

a. She has no money.

b. She doesn't like her teachers.

c. She is not used to life in the U.S.

2. Professor Saunders asks Samorn to stay at Brenton for ______.

a. one week

b. two weeks

c. one month

3. Why does Samorn start to enjoy herself at Brenton?

a. She can speak English better.

b. She makes some friends.

c. She finds a new boyfriend.

4. Why does Lek come to see Samorn?

a. He is on vacation.

b He wants to take her back to Thailand.

c. He wants to study at Brenton with her.

5. Why does Samorn decide not to go home in the end?

a. Lek doesn't want to marry her.

b. Lek will come to live in the U.S. with her.

c. She wants to finish her studies.

Answer Key

A: 1. c; 2. e; 3. b; 4. a; 5. f; 6. d

B: 1. different; 2. lawyer; 3. future; 4. dormitory; 5. nightclub; 6. presentation; 7. marry

C: 1. c; 2. a; 3. a; 4. b; 5. c

Background Reading:

Spotlight on . . . Studying Abroad

To study abroad means to live and study in another country for a period of time. It can be anything from a few weeks to a few years. If you are studying abroad or are thinking of it, you are not alone. Every year, millions of students leave their home countries to study abroad. Many agree that it can be a life-changing experience.

Studying abroad is a good way to . . .

- Learn a new language: There is no better way to master a language than to live in a place where it is spoken everywhere!
- Travel: Since studying abroad often puts you on a different continent, you are much closer to places you might not have had the opportunity to visit.
- Make friends from around the world: While abroad, you get to meet people from your host country as well as other international students just like yourself.
- Learn about another culture: The only way to really know a country's culture or people is to live there.
- Learn about yourself: Being thrown into a new culture is scary at first, but it's also exciting. It's an opportunity to discover new strengths and abilities. Students who study abroad also return home with new ideas and views about themselves and their own culture.

Finding the right school

- Do you want to go to a small or big college? Smaller colleges tend to be quieter and have fewer choices of courses. However, they tend to be more personal.
- What do you want to study? Does your college have this course? Choose the college that can give you the best education.
- Do you want to live in a big city or a small town? Smaller towns have fewer things to do, but are cheaper than big cities.
- Do you want to live in the college dorm, or share an apartment? Living in the dormitory is safer and usually cheaper, but there isn't as much freedom.
- Are you a sports person? Look out for sports facilities like a gym, running track, or sports teams you can join. If you are like arts and music, see if your college has a student theater or performing arts center.

Countries with the most international students (2006/07)

1. United States
   595,874 (20%)
2. United Kingdom
   351,470 (13%)
3. France
   246,612 (8%)
4. Australia
   211,526 (7%)
5. Germany
   206,875 (6.5%)

Background Reading:
Spotlight on . . . Homesickness

What is homesickness?

Like Samorn, many international students miss their family and homes. This is called feeling "homesick." For some, this feeling quickly disappears as they adapt to a new environment; for others, it takes a lot longer.

Beating homesickness

- Check out your new home. Visit your new university with your parents or friends at least once before you move there. That can make it easier when you actually move there.
- Bring something that reminds you of home. Pack photos, letters, or your favorite stuffed animal, pajamas, or pillow.
- Do something you enjoy. When you're having fun, you're less likely to spend time thinking about people and things you miss.
- Talk to a friend. Many students go through the same experience as you. Knowing you're not the only one dealing with this can make you feel better.
- Write in a diary. Putting your feelings down on paper can help you understand them.
- Talk to an adult. If you're having trouble eating or sleeping, talk to an adult you trust about your feelings. Many schools have trained staff to help students deal with being away from home.

Think About It

1. Have you ever studied overseas, or stayed in another country for a long period of time? How did you feel?
2. Imagine you are going to live in another country. What are some things you should find out before you go?

Glossary

airport	(*n.*)	the place you go to catch a plane
coach	(*n.*)	the manager of a sports team who helps the team
cry	(*v.*)	when water comes from your eyes because you are happy or sad
economics	(*n.*)	the study of money
dance	(*v.*)	move your body to music
dorm	(*n.*)	A dorm (dormitory) is a building where many students live.
funny	(*adj.*)	When something is funny, it makes you laugh.
future	(*n.*)	the time after now, e.g., next year
hurt	(*adj.*)	If a part of your body hurts, you feel pain there.
kiss	(*n. + v.*)	when two people put their lips together to express love
lawyer	(*n.*)	a person who can help you with or tell you about the law
loud	(*adj.*)	noisy
marry	(*v.*)	When two people marry, they become partners for life.
nightclub	(*n.*)	a place you can go dancing
presentation	(*n.*)	When you give a presentation, you talk to many people about something.
ready	(*adj.*)	If you get ready to go out, you put on your clothes.

stay	(*v.*)	If you stay in a place, you do not move from there.
team	(*n.*)	a group of players who play a sport together
tracksuit	(*n.*)	sports clothes
university	(*n.*)	a place to study after you finish high school
voice	(*n.*)	When you speak, someone hears your voice.